Pebble® Plus

LET'S LOOK AT COUNTRIES

LET'S LOOK AT

NORTH KOREA

BY JOY FRISCH-SCHMOLL

CAPSTONE PRESS
a capstone imprint

Pebble Plus is published by Capstone Press,
1710 Roe Crest Drive, North Mankato, Minnesota 56003
www.mycapstone.com

Library of Congress Cataloging-in-Publication Data
Names: Frisch-Schmoll, Joy, author.
Title: Let's look at North Korea / by Joy Frisch-Schmoll.
Description: North Mankato, Minnesota : Capstone Press, [2019] | Series: Pebble plus. Let's look at countries
Identifiers: LCCN 2018029939 (print) | LCCN 2018031062 (ebook) | ISBN 9781977103888 (eBook PDF) | ISBN 9781977103796 (hardcover) | ISBN 9781977105585 (pbk.)
Subjects: LCSH: Korea (North)—Juvenile literature.
Classification: LCC DS932 (ebook) | LCC DS932 .F75 2019 (print) | DDC 951.93—dc23
LC record available at https://lccn.loc.gov/2018029939

Editorial Credits
Erika L. Shores, editor; Juliette Peters, designer; Jo Miller, media researcher;
Laura Manthe, production specialist

Photo Credits
Dreamstime: Wanghanan, 21 (Top); Getty Images/AFP/KIM WON-JIN, 15; iStockphoto: Tae-young, 9; Shutterstock: Anton_Ivanov, 11, Astrelok, 13, Attila JANDI, Cover Middle, Cover Back, Chintung Lee, Cover Top, CJ Nattanai, 1, Globe Turner, 22 (Inset), Kanokratnok, 18, Lenard Zhukovsky, 17, Lukiyanova Natalia frenta, 22-23, 24, Matej Hudovernik, 5, 10, Mieszko9, 7, Munhee Choi, Cover Bottom, nate, 4, Nicolo' Pastorelli, 3, Ole_CNX, 19, Viktoria Gaman, 21 (Bottom)

Note to Parents and Teachers

The Let's Look at Countries set supports national curriculum standards for social studies related to people, places, and culture. This book describes and illustrates North Korea. The images support early readers in understanding the text. The repetition of words and phrases helps early readers learn new words. This book also introduces early readers to subject-specific vocabulary words, which are defined in the Glossary section. Early readers may need assistance to read some words and to use the Table of Contents, Glossary, Read More, Internet Sites, Critical Thinking Questions, and Index sections of the book.

Printed and bound in China.
970

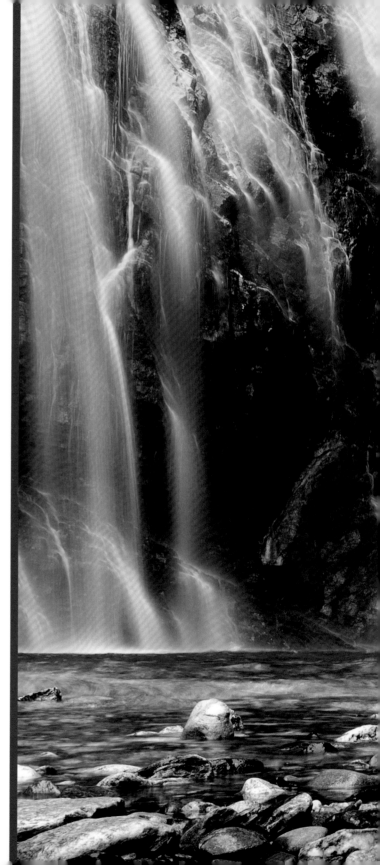

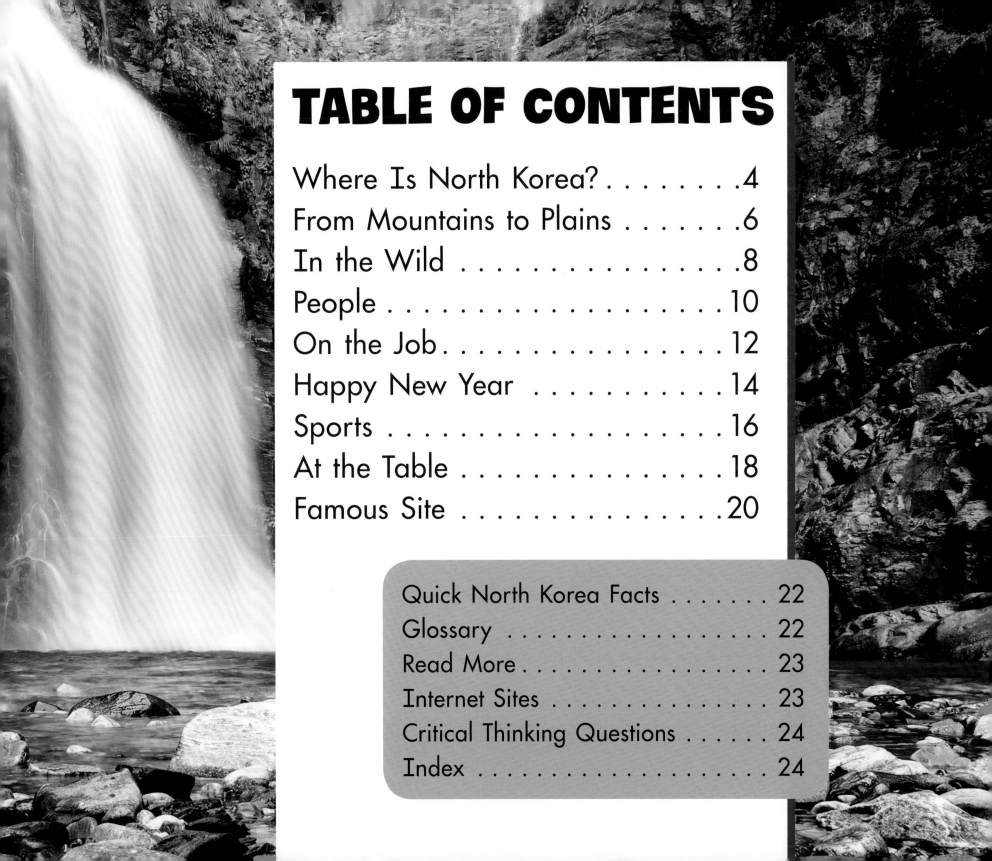

TABLE OF CONTENTS

Where Is North Korea?

North Korea is on a peninsula in eastern Asia. It is the size of the U.S. state of Pennsylvania. North Korea's capital city is Pyongyang.

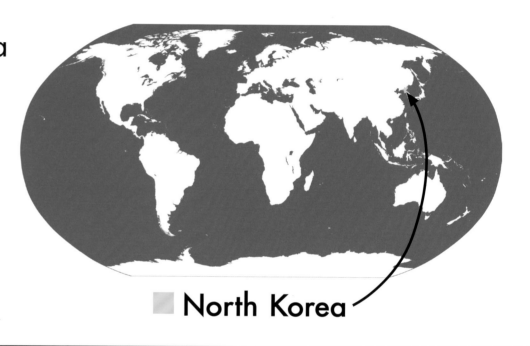

North Korea

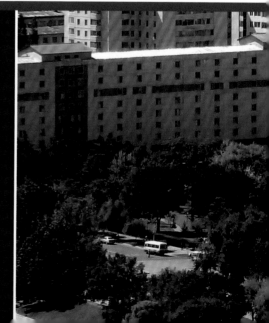

Pyongyang, North Korea

From Mountains to Plains

Mountains and valleys cover most of North Korea.

There are plains near the coasts.

Winters are long and cold.

Summers are hot and rainy.

7

In the Wild

Lynxes live in North Korea's woodlands.

These cats hunt deer and rabbits.

Wild goats eat grass on rocky hills.

Cranes catch fish along the coast.

cranes

People

Almost everyone in

North Korea is Korean.

Most people live in cities.

They live in apartments

in tall buildings.

On the Job

The government tells people where they will work. People have jobs in factories, mines, or on farms. Anyone 18 years old must serve in the military for up to 10 years.

Happy New Year

Seollal is the Korean New Year.

The holiday lasts three days.

Children fly kites and play games.

Families eat special foods and give gifts.

15

Sports

Jump! Kick! Spin!

Taekwondo began in North Korea.

Many children take lessons.

Gymnastics, table tennis, and

basketball are also popular sports.

At the Table

Rice and noodles are common foods in North Korea. Koreans eat soups and vegetables. Kimchi is popular. This dish is made with cabbage and spices.

kimchi

Famous Site

The Arirang Mass Games take

place at May Day Stadium.

Thousands of performers dance

and do gymnastics. Children hold up

cards to make giant pictures.

QUICK NORTH KOREA FACTS

North Korean flag

Name: Democratic People's Republic of Korea

Capital: Pyongyang

Other major cities: Hamhung, Chongjin, Nampo

Population: 25,248,140 (2017 estimate)

Size: 46,540 square miles (120,538 sq km)

Language: Korean

Money: Won

GLOSSARY

coast—land that is near the ocean

crane—a large water bird with long, thin legs and a long neck

government—the group of people that has power to make laws and important decisions

lynx—a wildcat that has soft, spotted fur, pointed ears, and a short tail

military—having to do with soldiers or armies

mine—a deep hole made in the earth so that coal and other minerals can be taken out

peninsula—a piece of land nearly surrounded on all sides by water

taekwondo—a form of Korean karate

READ MORE

Murray, Julie. *North Korea.* Explore the Countries. Minneapolis: ABDO Publishing Company, 2016.

O'Neal, Claire. *We Visit North Korea.* Your Land and My Land: Asia. Hockessin, Del.: Mitchell Lane Publishers, 2014.

Sonneborn, Liz. *North Korea.* Enchantment of the World. New York: Scholastic, 2014.

INTERNET SITES

Use FactHound to find Internet sites related to this book.

Visit *www.facthound.com*

Just type 9781977103796 and go.

Check out projects, games and lots more at
www.capstonekids.com

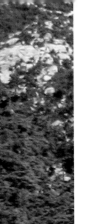

CRITICAL THINKING QUESTIONS

1. Describe how North Koreans celebrate the Korean New Year.

2. How would you feel if your government chose a job for you?

3. Which North Korean sport would you want to try? Why did you choose that one?

INDEX